Paragraph Writing
Grade 8

What makes you happy?

What makes you happy ?

Who do you like to play with the most ?

What animal do you give kisses to ?

What time of the day is your favorite ?

What relative is your favorite ?

What holiday is your favorite ?

Do you ever feel confused?

Do you ever feel confused ?

What is too hard for you ?

Have you ever steered a car ?

Have you ever filled up an entire journal ?

Have you ever started a computer ?

Have you ever gone shopping with your parents ?

Have you ever cooked a meal on the stove ?

Have you ever read an entire book ?

106 Printable Pages

C. Mahoney

Life is about choices...

What makes you happy?

What makes you
happy ?

Who do you like to
play with the most ?

What animal do you
give kisses to ?

What time of
the day is your
favorite ?

When are you
happiest ?

What relative is
your favorite ?

What holiday is
your favorite ?

What day of the
week is your favor-
ite ?

_____

_____

_____

_____

_____

_____

_____

_____

_____

_____

_____

Do you ever feel confused?

Do you ever feel confused ?

What is too hard for you ?

Have you ever steered a car ?

Have you ever filled up an entire journal ?

Have you ever started a computer ?

Have you ever gone shopping with your parents ?

Have you ever cooked a meal on the stove ?

Have you ever read an entire book ?

_____
_____
_____
_____
_____
_____
_____
_____
_____
_____
_____

What do you know about George Washington?

What do you know about George Washington ?

Did you know that he was a husband ?

Why did men wear wigs long ago ?

Would you like to be President one day ?

Why do men shave the hair from their faces ?

How can a president help the citizens of the country ?

What do you need to know in order to be President ?

Why do men wear jackets in the daytime ?

_____
_____
_____
_____
_____
_____
_____
_____
_____
_____
_____

English

turtle

Spanish

tortuga

(tohr-too-gah)

Are turtles brave?

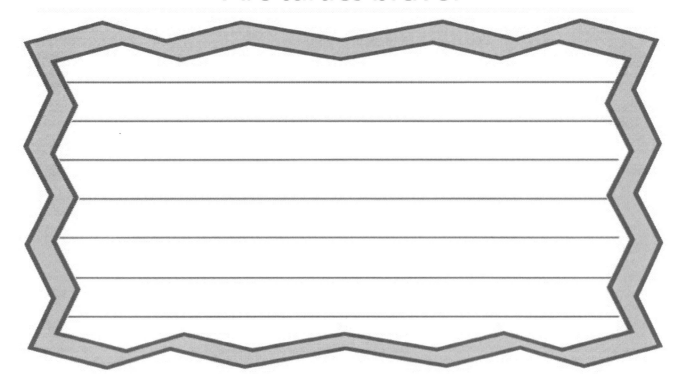

English
beetle

Spanish
escarabajo
(es-kahr-ah-bvah-hoh)

When does a beetle sleep?

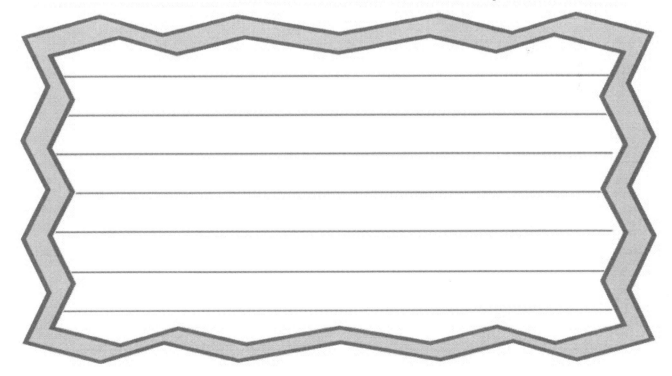

Why do we celebrate Christmas?

What is awesome about Christmas ?

Why would some-one get coal in their stocking ?

What shapes do you see on a Christmas tree ?

Do you cele-brate Christ-mas with a live tree or a fake tree ?

Do you help decorate the Christmas tree ?

What do you know about Santa Claus ?

Who is responsible for all of those pre-sents under a tree ?

When do your par-ents take down the Christmas tree ?

_____
_____
_____
_____
_____
_____
_____
_____
_____
_____
_____

Why do we celebrate Earth Day?

Is the Earth okay **?**

Where do the books that you read come from **?**

Where do the clothes that you wear come from **?**

Where does the air that you breathe come from **?**

EARTH DAY

APRIL 22

Where does the electricity that runs your lights come from **?**

Where does the food that you eat come from **?**

Where does the water that you drink come from **?**

Where does the gas that runs your car come from **?**

_____

_____

_____

_____

_____

_____

_____

_____

_____

_____

_____

Why is the desert hot?

_____
_____
_____
_____
_____
_____
_____
_____
_____
_____
_____
_____
_____

Why do rocks have lines and grooves?

_____
_____
_____
_____
_____
_____
_____
_____
_____
_____
_____
_____
_____

Why do we celebrate Easter?

What is Easter ?

What games do you play on Easter ?

Have you ever painted eggs on Easter ?

When is Easter celebrated ?

What words do you hear on Easter ?

Is candy good for you ?

What do bunnies have to do with Easter ?

What is your favorite Easter surprise ?

_____

_____

_____

_____

_____

_____

_____

_____

_____

_____

_____

Why do we celebrate Father's Day?

What is special
about your father?

What is a father's
biggest responsibil-
ity at home ?

Why do adults go to
work ?

Do you know
the first name
of your fa-
ther ?

SUPER

DAD

Why do chil-
dren hug or
kiss their fa-
ther ?

How do fathers
teach their children
how to be kind ?

Is it okay for adults
to hurt children ?

What are common
words your father
says ?

_____

_____

_____

_____

_____

_____

_____

_____

_____

_____

_____

English	**Spanish**
jellyfish	medusa
	(may-doo-sah)

How come jellyfish have no bones?

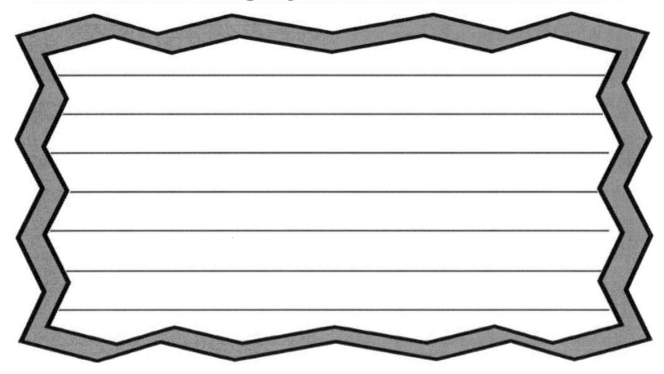

English

raccoon

Spanish

mapache
(mah-pah-chay)

Why does a raccoon have fur?

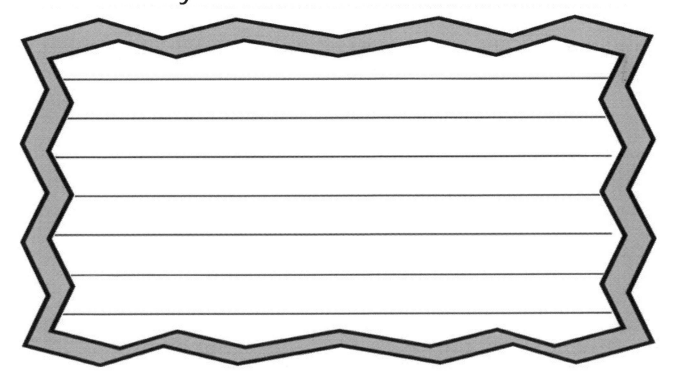

What is Special about the American Flag?

What does the flag look like ?

Is America kind to people from other countries ?

How can a foreigner come to the U.S. ?

What does respect really mean ?

Why is it important that immigrants enter our country legally ?

Why do Americans honor the Stars and Stripes ?

When is the last time you recited the Pledge of Allegience ?

How did you learn about America ?

_____

_____

_____

_____

_____

_____

_____

_____

_____

_____

_____

Why do we celebrate Black History Month?

When is Black History Month ?

What does "black" mean ?

What are other ways of saying "black" ?

How can people who are different like each other ?

Is it okay to identify someone by their skin color ?

Is it okay to talk about skin color ?

Is it okay to like someone who does not look like you ?

Is it okay to like someone who looks like you ?

_____
_____
_____
_____
_____
_____
_____
_____
_____
_____
_____

Why do birds have feathers?

_____
_____
_____
_____
_____
_____
_____
_____
_____
_____
_____
_____
_____

Why do people need to sit down?

_____
_____
_____
_____
_____
_____
_____
_____
_____
_____
_____
_____
_____

What Books Do You Like to Read?

Do you like to read ?

Do you have a book shelf in your bedroom ?

How many kid's books are in your bedroom ?

Is it possible to read too much ?

Do you subscribe to a kids magazine ?

Who is your favorite book character ?

What types of books do you like to read ?

How much time do you spend reading in your bedroom each day ?

_____
_____
_____
_____
_____
_____
_____
_____
_____
_____

What Is Your Favorite Board Game?

What is your favorite board game ?

How do you win a game ?

What are the rules of checkers ?

How important is winning to you ?

Is it okay to cheat in a game ?

What snacks do you like to eat when playing games with friends ?

How can you keep a gameboard clean ?

What happens if you don't want to play anymore ?

_____
_____
_____
_____
_____
_____
_____
_____
_____
_____
_____

English
chicken

Spanish
gallina
(gah-yee-nah)

Can a chicken really dance?

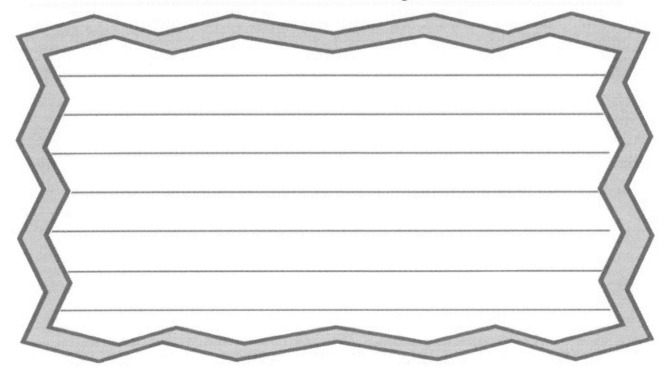

English

skunk

Spanish

mofeta

(moh-fay-tah)

Why does a skunk have a stripe?

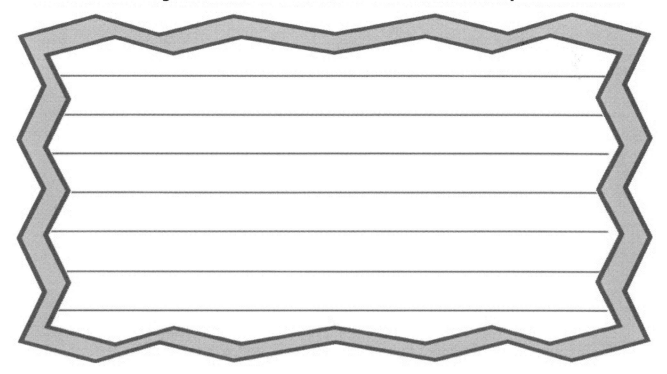

What Makes You Laugh?

What makes you laugh **?**

Who is the funniest person in your family **?**

Who is the funniest person on television **?**

Are you good at making other people laugh **?**

Who is the funniest person in your class **?**

What silly things make you laugh the hardest **?**

What parts of your body are involved in laughing **?**

Why do people laugh when someone does something silly **?**

_____
_____
_____
_____
_____
_____
_____
_____
_____
_____
_____
_____

What Do Your Eyes Do?

What are your eyes
made of ?

Why do your eyes
sometimes itch ?

Have you ever
been poked in the
eye with a finger ?

How can you
protect your
eyes when in
the sun ?

Have you ever
gotten a black
eye ?

Why do your eyes
get tired at night ?

What happens to
your eyes if you're
in the sun all day ?

How do your eyes
stay clean ?

_____
_____
_____
_____
_____
_____
_____
_____
_____
_____
_____

Why does the sky appear blue?

Do you mind being by yourself in the daytime?

_____

_____

_____

_____

_____

_____

_____

_____

What Do Your Ears Do?

Why do we have
ears ?

What does an ear
look like ?

How can you pro-
tect your ears ?

What is your
favorite song ?

What sounds
annoy you ?

What is the most
important rule about
hearing ?

What words do you
like to hear ?

Why are some chil-
dren unable to hear
sounds ?

_____

_____

_____

_____

_____

_____

_____

_____

_____

_____

_____

What Does Your Tongue Do?

What is the purpose of the tongue ?

What are you not allowed to do with your tongue at school ?

Is it okay to stick your tongue at someone ?

What flavor does your tongue like best ?

Why does the tongue always feel wet ?

What happens to your tongue when you eat something spicy ?

What happens to your tongue when you eat ice-cream ?

What happens to your tongue when you eat a lollipop ?

_____

_____

_____

_____

_____

_____

_____

_____

_____

_____

_____

English

pig

Spanish

cerdo

(sayr-doh)

Can a pig really read a book?

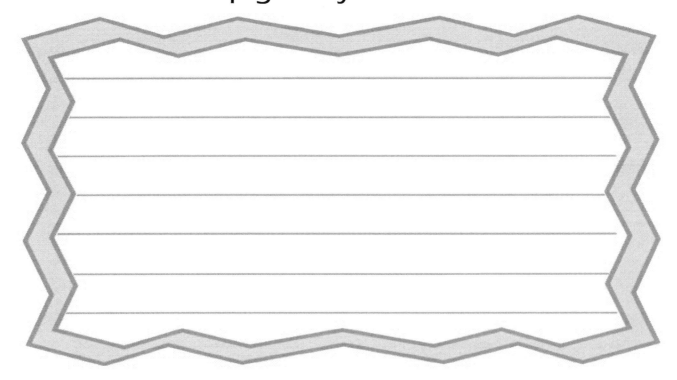

English

deer

Spanish

ciervo

(see-ayr-voh)

Why is a deer easily frightened?

What Does Your Nose Do?

What is your nose for ?

Why do people put deodorant on their armpits ?

Why do people put air freshener in a restroom ?

Why do people wear perfume or cologne ?

What brown things smell horrible ?

What wet things smell fantastic ?

What food has no smell at all ?

What invisible things smell horrible ?

_____
_____
_____
_____
_____
_____
_____
_____
_____
_____

What Does Your Skin Do?

Why does our skin sweat ?

Why do we stink when we exercise ?

Why do clothes stink after wearing them ?

What should you do if you feel sick while sweating ?

How can you keep cool in the sun's heat ?

Is it dangerous to sweat too much ?

How does drinking water help you when you're hot ?

What color clothes help to keep you cool ?

_____
_____
_____
_____
_____
_____
_____
_____
_____
_____
_____

What is your earliest memory as a kid?

Is it okay to hate someone and wish that they were dead?

_____

_____

_____

_____

_____

_____

_____

_____

What Are Your Feet For?

Why do people run ?

What is the fastest animal on land ?

Is running healthy for you ?

What sports involve running ?

When is it not okay to run ?

Is running dangerous ?

Is it easier to run uphill or downhill ?

Have you ever run away from someone ?

_____
_____
_____
_____
_____
_____
_____
_____
_____
_____
_____

What Do You Dream About?

What do you dream about ?

Why do we need to sleep at night ?

Have you ever slept on a couch ?

Do you sleep alone or with a stuffed animal ?

Do you have a room all to yourself ?

How do you fall asleep ?

What is your mind doing while you sleep ?

When is the last time you got scared of thunder ?

_____
_____
_____
_____
_____
_____
_____
_____
_____
_____

English

woodpecker

Spanish

pájaro carpintero
(pah-hah-roh cahr-peen-tay-roh)

How does a woodpecker find bugs?

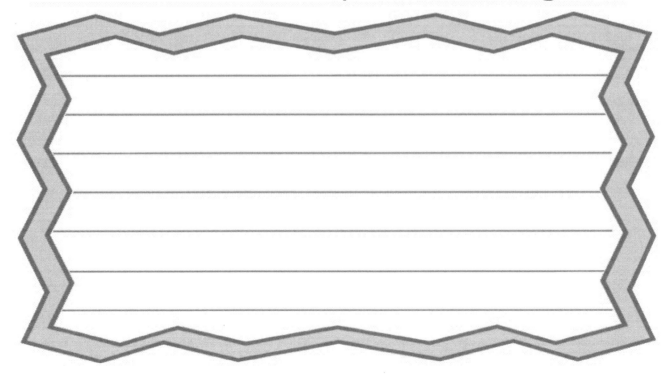

English

mosquito

Spanish

mosquito

(mohs-kee-toh)

Why do mosquitos like humans?

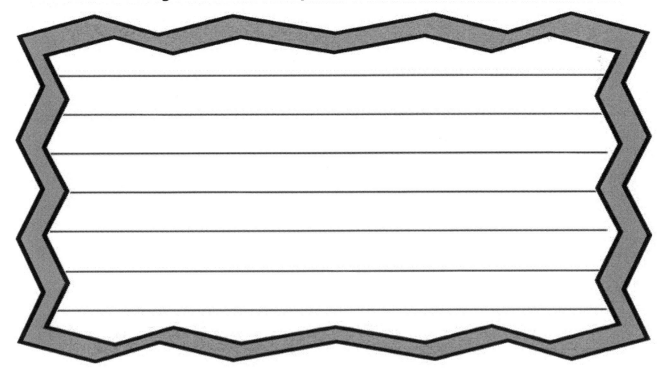

Where Do You Like to Hide?

Do you like to play Hide-and-Seek ?

Where is the best place to hide inside your house ?

Where is the best place to hide out- side in your yard ?

What is the most important rule in the game Hide- and-Seek ?

Where is the best place to hide at school ?

Where is the best place to hide at your grandma's house ?

Where is the best place to hide at a city park ?

Where is the best place to hide in a store ?

_____

_____

_____

_____

_____

_____

_____

_____

_____

_____

_____

_____

Have You Ever...?

Have you ever
played the drums ?

Have you ever eat-
en a snail ?

Have you ever bro-
ken a shoe string ?

Have you ever
crushed a so-
da can ?

Have you ever
thrown a pine
cone ?

Have you ever
thrown a rock in the
water ?

Have you ever held
a butterfly ?

Have you ever
caught a lizard ?

_____

_____

_____

_____

_____

_____

_____

_____

_____

_____

WHY IS IT IMPORTANT TO EXERCISE EVERY DAY?

_____

_____

_____

_____

_____

_____

_____

What happens to a leaf that falls to the ground?

_____

_____

_____

_____

_____

_____

_____

_____

What Card Games Do You Like to Play?

What do you like about cards ?

What games can you play with cards ?

What does a playing card look like ?

Is it okay to cheat at cards ?

How do you feel when you lose a game of cards ?

What is the most important rule about cards ?

When is the last time you played with cards ?

What card is your favorite in the deck ?

_____

_____

_____

_____

_____

_____

_____

_____

_____

_____

_____

What Does Your Hair Look Like?

What is the purpose of hair ?

Why do people shampoo their hair ?

Do you use a comb or a brush on your hair ?

What color hair do you have ?

Why don't more girls shave off all their hair ?

Why do people shave off their body hair ?

How does the hair on your arms and legs feel ?

Why does hair grow in the nose and ears ?

_____

_____

_____

_____

_____

_____

_____

_____

_____

_____

_____

Why do people wear make-up and fancy clothes and jewelry?

_____

_____

_____

_____

_____

_____

_____

_____

Is it okay to call someone or something "stupid"?

_____

_____

_____

_____

_____

_____

_____

_____

What Do Your Eyes Look Like?

Why are eyes different colors?

What color are your eyes ?

Why do people wear sunglasses ?

Is it okay to stare at someone ?

Why do old people need reading glasses ?

Why do we have tears ?

Why do we blink ?

Why do our eyes turn red sometimes ?

_____
_____
_____
_____
_____
_____
_____
_____
_____
_____
_____

What Does Love Mean?

Why do people
make a heart sign ?

What does your
heart inside your
chest actually do ?

Where do feelings
come from ?

Who loves
you ?

What are
some good
feelings ?

How can you let
someone know that
you don't like them ?

How can you let
someone know that
you like them ?

What are some bad
feelings ?

_____

_____

_____

_____

_____

_____

_____

_____

_____

_____

_____

What do you know about <u>flies</u>?

_____
_____
_____
_____
_____
_____
_____
_____
_____
_____
_____
_____
_____
_____
_____

What do you know about <u>jumping spiders</u>?

_____
_____
_____
_____
_____
_____
_____
_____
_____
_____
_____
_____
_____
_____
_____
_____

Your Backpack

What colors are on the outside of your backpack **?**

How many zippers does your backpack have **?**

How many pockets does your backpack have **?**

Do you have a cell phone in your back-pack **?**

Do you carry a water bottle in your back-pack **?**

Do you carry house keys in your back-pack **?**

How many pencils are in your back-pack right now **?**

How many books are in your back-pack right now **?**

_____
_____
_____
_____
_____
_____
_____
_____
_____
_____
_____

What do you know about cameras?

What is a video camera made of ?

Where do video cameras come from ?

How does a video camera remember what it sees ?

What funny things have your parents recorded of you ?

How do you keep a camera clean ?

What happens if you steal some-thing ?

Why do stores have cameras in them ?

Is it okay to take videos of other peo-ple ?

_____
_____
_____
_____
_____
_____
_____
_____
_____
_____
_____

What do you know about <u>tree frogs</u>?

_____

_____

_____

_____

_____

_____

_____

_____

_____

_____

_____

_____

_____

_____

What do you know about <u>caterpillars?</u>

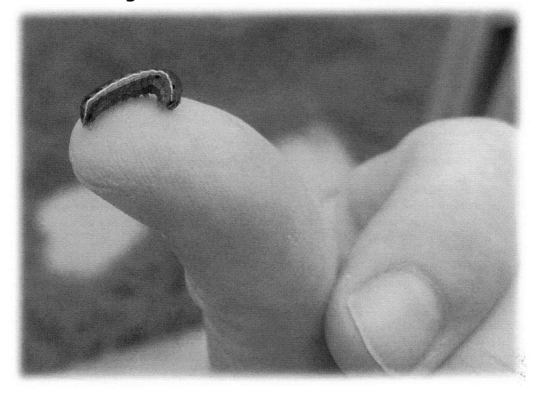

_____

_____

_____

_____

_____

_____

_____

_____

_____

_____

_____

_____

_____

_____

_____

_____

_____

What is Fun about Baseball?

What is a base-ball ?

What is a bat ?

What is the job of a pitcher ?

Why do play-ers wear uni-forms ?

What is the job of a catcher ?

What is the job of a coach ?

What is the job of a fielder ?

What is the job of a batter ?

_____
_____
_____
_____
_____
_____
_____
_____
_____
_____
_____
_____

What is Fun about Football?

What is the purpose of football **?**

What safety equipment is most important in this sport **?**

Can boys and girls both be football players **?**

Can a game end in a tie **?**

How many points is a touchdown **?**

What happens if you fumble the ball **?**

What happens if you intercept the ball **?**

How many points is a field goal**?**

_____
_____
_____
_____
_____
_____
_____
_____
_____
_____

What do you know about lady bugs?

_____
_____
_____
_____
_____
_____
_____
_____
_____
_____
_____
_____
_____
_____
_____
_____

What do you know about <u>water</u>?

_____
_____
_____
_____
_____
_____
_____
_____
_____
_____
_____
_____
_____
_____
_____
_____
_____

Boys and Girls...

How are boys and girls different ?

Why do girls have long hair ?

Why do boys give girls flowers ?

How are boys and girls the same ?

Can boys and girls play to-gether ?

What kind of shoes do boys and girls wear ?

Why do girls wear ribbons in their hair ?

Why do girls wear skirts and dresses ?

_____
_____
_____
_____
_____
_____
_____
_____
_____
_____
_____

Ants...

What is an ant made of ?

Where might you see ants ?

Are ants important for the Earth ?

What does an ant look like ?

How does an ant move from one place to another ?

What is the most important rule about ants ?

How is an ant different from a spider ?

Why do adults kill ants in the kitchen ?

_____

_____

_____

_____

_____

_____

_____

_____

_____

_____

How does a spider stay safe?

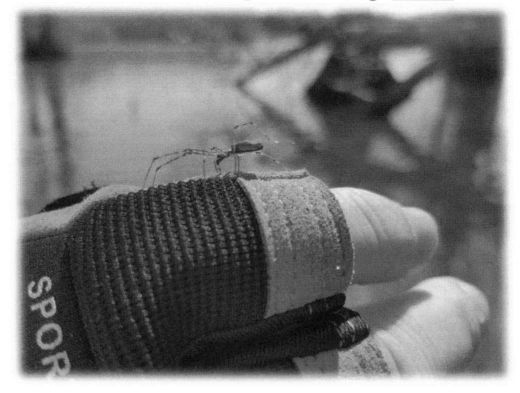

_____
_____
_____
_____
_____
_____
_____
_____
_____
_____
_____
_____
_____
_____
_____

How does a leaf know what <u>shape</u> to take?

_____
_____
_____
_____
_____
_____
_____
_____
_____
_____
_____
_____
_____
_____
_____
_____

Spiders...

What is a spider made of **?**

Are spiders safe to hold **?**

How does a spider move **?**

Where do spiders go when it rains **?**

What do spiders eat **?**

What is the most important rule about spiders **?**

How is a spider different from a caterpillar **?**

Are spiders good or bad **?**

_____

_____

_____

_____

_____

_____

_____

_____

_____

_____

Snails...

What is a snail
made of ?

Are snails fun to
hold ?

How does a snail
move ?

Where do
snails go when
it is hot out-
side ?

What do snails
eat ?

What is the most
important rule about
snails ?

How is a
snail different from
a worm ?

Are snails good or
bad ?

_____
_____
_____
_____
_____
_____
_____
_____
_____
_____
_____

Where does <u>dirt</u> come from?

_____
_____
_____
_____
_____
_____
_____
_____
_____
_____
_____
_____
_____
_____
_____
_____

What is a bee's <u>purpose</u> in life?

_____
_____
_____
_____
_____
_____
_____
_____
_____
_____
_____
_____
_____
_____
_____
_____

Beetles...

What do you know about beetles **?**

What does a beetle do all day **?**

Where might you find a beetle **?**

What does a beetle look like **?**

Are beetle dangerous **?**

What animals might eat a beetle **?**

How does a beetle find food to eat **?**

How do beetles protect themselves from hungry predators **?**

_____

_____

_____

_____

_____

_____

_____

_____

_____

_____

_____

Snakes...

What is a snake ?

What animals are afraid of snakes ?

Where can you find a snake ?

Have you ever touched a snake ?

What does a snake need in order to survive ?

What is the most important rule about snakes ?

What does a snake look like ?

How does a snake protect itself from hungry critters ?

_____

_____

_____

_____

_____

_____

_____

_____

_____

_____

_____

What confuses you?

WHY IS REST IMPORTANT?

_____

_____

_____

_____

_____

_____

_____

_____

OK

What Sports Do You Like to Play?

What sports do you like to play ?

Why is good for your body to exercise ?

Which emotions do you feel when you play a sport with a friend ?

How does playing sports help you learn about yourself ?

How does it feel to lose a sport's game ?

What do coaches tell athletes to do after a game ?

Is it okay to insult opponents ?

What is the most important rule for sports ?

_____
_____
_____
_____
_____
_____
_____
_____
_____
_____
_____

What Video Games Do You Like to Play?

What games do you have at home ?

Is it more fun watch tv or to play a video game on the tv ?

What words do you say when playing a video game ?

Do you have video games in your bedroom ?

What part of your body gets tired when you play video games ?

Is it okay to play video games where characters steal things ?

Is it okay to play video games where characters kill each other ?

Is it okay to play video games where characters say rude things ?

_____
_____
_____
_____
_____
_____
_____
_____
_____
_____
_____

How does a leaf get so many holes?

_____
_____
_____
_____
_____
_____
_____
_____
_____
_____
_____
_____
_____
_____

What is a pine cone?

What Do You Know about Donald Trump?

What do you know about Donald Trump ?

Did you know that he is a husband and a father ?

Should a President listen to the advice of experts ?

Is it okay to insult people and call them names ?

Is it okay to lie in order to get what you want ?

How can a president help the citizens of the country ?

What should you be good at if you are the President ?

How can a president help immigrants from other countries ?

_____
_____
_____
_____
_____
_____
_____
_____
_____
_____
_____
_____

What Do You Know about Video Games?

Have you ever played a video game all by yourself ?

What part of your body gets the most action ?

What is the goal of a video game ?

Why do people play games like this ?

Is an adult better at video games than a child ?

How much time are you allowed to play video games ?

What does this game sound like when it's being played ?

Does this game involve luck or skill ?

_____

_____

_____

_____

_____

_____

_____

_____

_____

_____

What do you like about flowers?

_____

_____

_____

_____

_____

_____

_____

_____

_____

_____

_____

Why do people need to sit down?

_____
_____
_____
_____
_____
_____
_____
_____
_____
_____
_____

What Do You Know about Water?

What is water **?**

Where does water come from **?**

How do cities make the water clean enough to drink **?**

What does water look like **?**

Is it safe to drink water from a lake or river **?**

What is the most important rule about water **?**

Why do humans need water **?**

How do people put pipes into the ground **?**

_____
_____
_____
_____
_____
_____
_____
_____
_____
_____
_____
_____

What Do You Know about Work?

Why do we have money ?

What does money sound like ?

Where does money come from ?

Why do people save money ?

How do you keep money clean ?

What happens if you steal some-thing ?

Who pays for the things you want in a store ?

Why do adults work ?

_____

_____

_____

_____

_____

_____

_____

_____

_____

_____

_____

What Do You Know about Cars?

How do cars hurt
the environment ?

Are cars safe ?

What do you do
while inside a car ?

What is a car
made of ?

When is the
last time that
you fell asleep
inside a car ?

What are the top
safety rules for rid-
ing inside a car ?

What is the purpose
of a car ?

Why can't children
drive cars ?

_____

_____

_____

_____

_____

_____

_____

_____

_____

_____

What causes shadows?

_____
_____
_____
_____
_____
_____
_____
_____
_____
_____
_____

Why are some flowers yellow?

Where Does Anger Come From?

Where does anger come from ?

What happens to your face when you get angry ?

How can you keep your anger from turning into vio-lence ?

Do animals get angry at other animals, or hu-mans ?

What makes you angry ?

Who did you get angry at most re-cently ?

Is it okay to get an-gry with someone ?

Why is it important not to say mean things when you are angry ?

_____
_____
_____
_____
_____
_____
_____
_____
_____
_____

What Are You Afraid Of?

What are you afraid of ?

Are you brave enough to let a spider crawl across your arm ?

Why are so many people afraid of spiders ?

Are spiders afraid of humans ?

Which spider is most dangerous to children ?

Where do spiders live ?

Why do spiders have fangs and poison ?

What do you know about spiders ?

_____

_____

_____

_____

_____

_____

_____

_____

_____

_____

_____

Where do clouds come from?

_____
_____
_____
_____
_____
_____
_____
_____
_____
_____
_____
_____
_____

How does a bug learn to fly?

_____
_____
_____
_____
_____
_____
_____
_____
_____
_____
_____

What do you like about your body?

Is your body amaz-
ing, or what ?

What do you like
about your feet ?

What do you like
about your hands ?

What do you
like about your
mind ?

What do you
like about your
hair ?

What do you like
about your skin ?

What do you like
about your mus-
cles ?

What do you like
about your eyes ?

_____
_____
_____
_____
_____
_____
_____
_____
_____
_____
_____

Do clowns make you laugh?

What does a clown look like ?

What games does a clown play ?

Why do clowns wear such colorful clothes ?

What would a clown do if you didn't laugh ?

How do clowns make you laugh ?

What words might a clown say ?

What kinds of tricks can a clown do ?

Where might you see a clown ?

_____

_____

_____

_____

_____

_____

_____

_____

_____

_____

_____

_____

When is the last time you hiked a trail alone?

_____
_____
_____
_____
_____
_____
_____
_____
_____
_____
_____
_____
_____
_____

Does a tree feel pain?

_____

_____

_____

_____

_____

_____

_____

_____

_____

_____

_____

_____

Why Do We Celebrate Groundhog Day?

What do you know about groundhogs ?

What causes shadows ?

What is fun about the winter ?

What is your favorite Saturday activity ?

How do flowers grow ?

Do you like the morning or evening better ?

How far can you see ?

Why is it hotter in the summer than in the winter ?

_____

_____

_____

_____

_____

_____

_____

_____

_____

_____

_____

English

parrot

Spanish

loro

(loh-roh)

What does a parrot sound like?

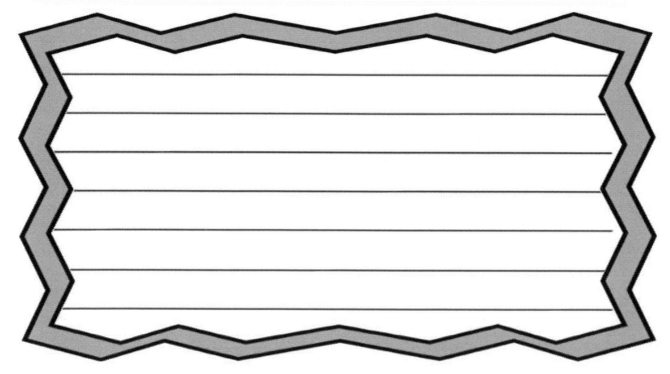

Snakes...

Where would you see a snake warning sign ?

Are all snakes dangerous ?

What should you do if you see a snake ?

Why do snakes try to get away from you when you are near ?

CAUTION
WATCH OUT FOR SNAKES

What do dogs do when they see or hear a snake ?

What should you do if you are bit by a venomous snake ?

Is it okay to pick up a non-venomous snake ?

Why does a rattlesnake make noise with its tail ?

_____
_____
_____
_____
_____
_____
_____
_____
_____
_____
_____

Squirrels...

What do you know about the squirrel ?

What other animals look similar to a squirrel ?

Where does a squirrel sleep at night ?

What predators prey on squirrels ?

How do squirrels find food to eat ?

Is it okay to feed squirrels snacks that humans eat ?

Is a squirrel dangerous to humans ?

What does a squirrel do when it senses danger ?

_____
_____
_____
_____
_____
_____
_____
_____
_____
_____
_____

Why Do We Celebrate Christmas?

What is awesome about Christmas ?

Why would some-one get coal in their stocking ?

What shapes do you see on a Christmas tree ?

Do you cele-brate Christ-mas with a live tree or a fake tree ?

Do you help decorate the Christmas tree ?

What do you know about Santa Claus ?

Who is responsible for all of those pre-sents under a tree ?

When do your par-ents take down the Christmas tree ?

_____

_____

_____

_____

_____

_____

_____

_____

_____

_____

What is special about the Christmas holiday?

What is special about Christmas ?

Who is this little baby ?

Why are there animals nearby ?

How are parents important to a baby ?

Have you ever slept with any animals ?

Why do we still tell this story to kids ?

What does straw feel like ?

Is a manger or barn a safe place to sleep ?

_____
_____
_____
_____
_____
_____
_____
_____
_____
_____
_____

Turtles...

What does a turtle
do all day **?**

Why do turtles hide
inside their shells **?**

How fast is a turtle **?**

What are turtles afraid of **?**

Have you ever
touched a turtle's shell **?**

Where do turtles
live **?**

What do turtles
eat **?**

Are turtles dangerous **?**

_____
_____
_____
_____
_____
_____
_____
_____
_____
_____

Whales...

What do you know about a whale ?

Where does a whale live ?

What does a whale eat ?

How does a whale move around ?

Is a whale big enough to swallow a human ?

Have you ever seen a living whale in the ocean ?

What does a whale do all day ?

What animals are afraid of the whale ?

_____
_____
_____
_____
_____
_____
_____
_____
_____
_____
_____

What is the purpose of a Christmas stocking?

Does your family use Christmas stockings **?**

Where might you hang a Christmas stocking **?**

Who puts stuff in your stocking **?**

Have you ever made your own stocking **?**

What little presents might you put in your parents' stockings **?**

What might you put in a pet's stocking **?**

Do you have a stocking for your dog or cat **?**

Is it okay to eat candy on Christmas day **?**

_____

_____

_____

_____

_____

_____

_____

_____

_____

_____

_____

_____

Why do people decorate evergreen trees inside their homes?

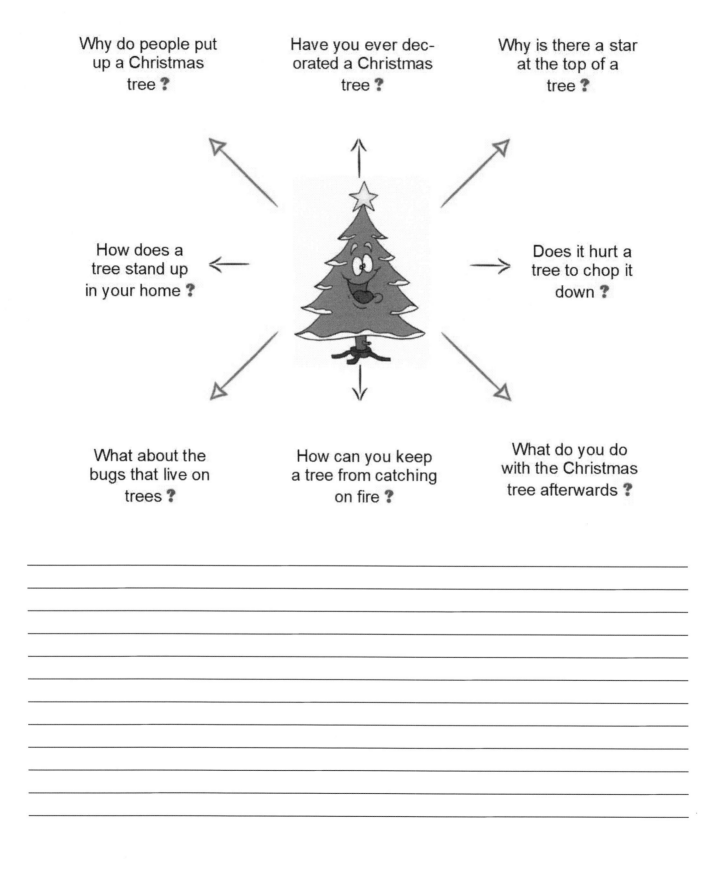

Why do people put up a Christmas tree ?

Have you ever decorated a Christmas tree ?

Why is there a star at the top of a tree ?

How does a tree stand up in your home ?

Does it hurt a tree to chop it down ?

What about the bugs that live on trees ?

How can you keep a tree from catching on fire ?

What do you do with the Christmas tree afterwards ?

_____

_____

_____

_____

_____

_____

_____

_____

_____

_____

_____

Woodpeckers...

What do you know about a woodpeck-er ?

What does this bird eat ?

What dangers does a bird face at night ?

What does this bird look like ?

How do birds stand on a wire without falling over ?

Have you ever held a bird ?

Which insect might a bird leave alone ?

What animals are smaller than this bird ?

_____

_____

_____

_____

_____

_____

_____

_____

_____

_____

_____

_____

Hot, Hot, Hot

What fun things can you do when it is hot ?

Why don't kids go to school in the summer ?

What is your favorite flavored popsicle ?

Where does the Sun go at night ?

Is soda good for you ?

How does the Sun stay warm ?

Why does the skin turn red when it has been in the Sun ?

Where does sweat come from ?

_____

_____

_____

_____

_____

_____

_____

_____

_____

_____

_____

What Is a Tornado?

What is a tornado ?

Where does the wind come from ?

How is a tornado dangerous ?

What types of weather scare you ?

How can you stay safe if there is a tornado approaching ?

What is the wind made of ?

Have you ever seen a tornado in real life ?

How do animals stay safe when a tornado comes ?

_____

_____

_____

_____

_____

_____

_____

_____

_____

_____

_____

Cell Phones and You

Are cell phones
dangerous ?

Why is it a bad idea
to walk while tex-
ting ?

Why is it a bad idea
to drive while tex-
ting ?

Is a cell phone
good or bad ?

Is it okay to
text someone
else while you
are eating din-
ner ?

How do cell phones
entertain you ?

How do cell phones
let you know what
to wear outside ?

How do cell phones
keep you safe ?

_____
_____
_____
_____
_____
_____
_____
_____
_____
_____
_____

Why do people decorate their homes with lights?

What do you know about decorating ?

Have you ever decorated a Christmas tree ?

Where does electricity come from ?

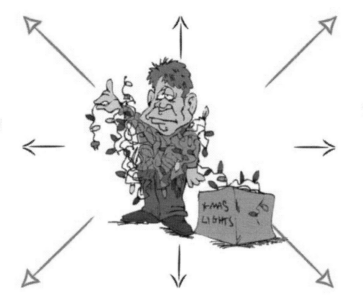

When do you put away Christmas stuff ?

Where does your family store the Christmas stuff ?

Do you like blinking lights or non-blinking lights ?

Why do people put lights outside their homes at Christmas ?

What colors do you see at Christmas ?

_____

_____

_____

_____

_____

_____

_____

_____

_____

_____

_____

Why do we give presents at Christmas?

Why do people give presents on Christmas ?

Why do we wrap presents ?

Does your family take turns with presents ?

What happens if a present breaks ?

Why are there bows on presents ?

Do your parents hide the presents from you ?

Is it okay to shake a present to find out what it is ?

How long does it take to wrap a present ?

_____

_____

_____

_____

_____

_____

_____

_____

_____

_____

_____

Spanish Pronunciation Guide

When you find "a" in a Spanish word, pronounce it /**ah**/ like *Pa, stop, bought*

When you find "e" in a Spanish word, pronounce it /**ay**/ like *play, straight, ate*

When you find "i" in a Spanish word, pronounce it /**ee**/ like *see, read, believe*

When you find "o" in a Spanish word, pronounce it /**oh**/ like *no, flow, toe*

When you find "u" in a Spanish word, pronounce it /**oo**/ like *flute, suit, root*

When you find "ai" in a Spanish word, pronounce it /**ay**/ like *straight*

When you find "ei" in a Spanish word, pronounce it /**ie**/ like *try, flight, kite*

When you find "b" in a Spanish word, pronounce it /**bv**/, quickly saying both.

When you find "c" in a Spanish word, pronounce it /**s**/ if it is ce- or ci-, and pronounce it /**k**/, if it is ca-, co- or cu-.

When you find "g" in a Spanish word, pronounce it /**h**/ if it is ge- or gi-, and pronounce it /**g**/, if it is ga-, go- or gu-.

When you find "gu" in a Spanish word, pronounce it /**gw**/ like *penguin*.

When you find "h" in a Spanish word, it is silent (except ch) like *honest*.

When you find "j" in a Spanish word, pronounce it /**h**/ like *hello*.

When you find "ll" in a Spanish word, pronounce it /**y**/ like *yes*.

When you find "ñ" in a Spanish word, pronounce it /**ny**/ like the Russian *nyet*.

When you find "rr" in a Spanish word, pronounce it /**rr**/, doubling the r, letting it roll or vibrate on your tongue.

When you find "z" in a Spanish word, pronounce it /**s**/, like *see*.

When you see an accent on a vowel (á, é, í, ó or ú), emphasize that syllable when you say the word.

46534599R00061

Made in the USA
Lexington, KY
28 July 2019